Recipes of A Young

SOUTHERN WIFE

Emily Roberts

Purpose Publishing

1503 Main Street #168 ♨ Grandview, Missouri
www.purposepublishing.com
Copyright © 2016 Emily Roberts

ISBN: 978-0692890783

Editing by Esile Potter

Printed in the United States of America.

First Edition published 2015
Revised Edition 2017

Contents

Desserts

About the Author

Introduction

Hi, I'm Emily Roberts and you may recognize me from my blog *Life of a Southern Wife* and if not, check it out at: http://lifeofasouthernwoman.weebly.com/

I've decided to write a recipe book for you to have at home. You may not know this but, I've been cooking since I was 15. And I love it! I enjoy cooking for my loved ones. What made me decide to start a blog was when my fiancée's brother got married, his young bride wasn't very experienced in the kitchen. So, I did what my mama did for me. I made her a cook book, but I didn't finish it. I wanted her to fill the rest with her own recipes. I'm now 21 and I've barely made a dent in my book. But I'm here to tell you any young lady can cook.

Entrees

Let's start off with something fairly simple shall we?

Chicken Fried Steak

A great southern dish. Tenderized beef steak with a crunchy breading and smothered in warm country gravy. This can be a great breakfast meal when complemented with eggs, hash-browns, and of course orange juice or coffee. This can also be a great dinner dish when served with mash potatoes and vegetables. This great treat to enjoy together with your family.

Prep & cook time: 20 minutes

2 lb round beef steak, cut into serving pieces
½ cup of flour
salt
groundpepper
½ teaspoon garlic powder
2 ½ cups milk
¼ cup vegetable oil

Pound round steak with meat mallet to tenderize. Combine flour, salt, pepper, and garlic powder, in a shallow bowl. Pour ½ cup of milk into another bowl. Heat oil in a large skillet over medium-high heat.

Dip steak into milk, then coat with flour mixture, shaking off excess flour, add steak to hot oil, and cook for 5 minutes or until brown, turn and brown on the remaining side. Remove the steak and keep it warm. (I usually use a package for the gravy).

Sticky Chicken

A yummy lip smacking meal the whole family is sure to love.

3 cups all-purpose flour
Salt and pepper to taste
4 lbs. of chicken breast (boneless and skinless)
½ cup of oil
2 envelopes of Lipton onion soup
2 (28 oz.) cans of stewed tomatoes
2 cups dry white wine

In a Ziploc bag add chicken, flour, salt and pepper, close tightly and shake to mix.

Heat oil in a skillet and brown the chicken. In a bowl combine soup mix, tomatoes, and wine; let stand while browning chicken.

Put chicken in two 9x13-inch dishes. Pour sauce mixture over chicken and bake for 1 to 1 ¼ hours at 325 degrees F. This good served with rice or just a veggie and a salad.

Homemade Meatloaf

My dad used to make this all the time when we were kids and we would devour it.

2 lbs. Of ground beef
1 cup of oatmeal oats
2 eggs
1 cup of salsa
1 tablespoon honey
1 1/2 of ketchup

In a large bowl mix together the ground beef, oatmeal, eggs, salsa until in a smooth ball. Line a bread pan with foil and spray with non-stick spray. Take your meat mixture and place it into the bread pan. Add the honey on top and cover with foil and bake in the oven at 400 degrees f for 1 hour 45 minutes. Take foil off of the top and add ketchup on top and put back in to the oven for the last ten minutes. Serves 6.

Loaded Baked Potato Soup

This is a yummy twist on potato soup. I love making this on a rainy day.

8 Medium baked potatoes
3/4 cups flour
3/4 cup melted butter
6 cups milk
1 lb. bacon fried crisp and crumbled
1 1/2 to 2 cups shredded cheddar cheese
4 green onions, chopped
1 chicken bouillon cube
8 oz. sour cream
Salt and pepper to taste

Bake potatoes, cook and cut into small cubes. Cook bacon until crisp, drain, cool, and crumble. Melt butter, add flour and cook, stir for 1 minute. Whisk in milk. Add bouillon cube. Add all ingredients except for sour cream. Heat through. When all hot, and then stir in sour cream.

Sheppard's Pie

This hearty all in one dish is good when you are short on funds, and is sure to impress the Meat and Potatoes guy in your life.

6-8 medium size potatoes
1 lb. ground beef
1 1/2 cup of shredded cheese
1 tablespoon Cajun seasoning of your choice
dash of salt and pepper
2 tablespoons of butter
1/2 cup of milk

Boil potatoes until soft when a knife inserts through them. Mash them up; add butter, salt& pepper, and milk. Stir until creamy. Brown ground beef, drain. Add Cajun seasoning. Pour into a 2 quart casserole dish, spread potatoes on top of the ground beef and top with cheese. Put in to the oven 300 degrees to melt the cheese.

Chicken and Rice Casserole

A simple and spicy homemade treat

2 leg quarters
1 cups rice
1/4 cup of onions
1/4 cup of salsa
2 chopped jalapeno peppers
Dash cayenne pepper
1 tablespoons Cajun seasoning
Dash of salt and pepper

Boil chicken until inside is done. Set aside to cool off. Boil rice in chicken broth until tender. Add salt, pepper, and jalapenos. Sauté onions in salsa and pour over rice mixture. Stir well and set aside. Debone chicken and combine with rice mixture. Pour in a baking dish and top with cheese. Bake at 450 degrees until cheese melts. Ready to serve.

Stuffed Bell Peppers

My aunt used to make these when we were kids. The peppers were always so juicy and cheesy.

Yields 4
1 lb. ground beef
2 bell peppers (color of your choice)
4 slices of American sliced cheese

Salt and pepper to taste. Slice peppers in half and clean out core and seeds, place peppers in a 9 x 13 baking dish and set aside. In a saucepan brown the ground beef and add salt and pepper to taste. Using a spoon scoop up the ground beef and place in the pepper, add as much or as little as desired. Top peppers with cheese and in to oven at 350 degrees until cheese is melted.

Stage Coach Chicken

2/3 cup ranch dressing
1 egg slightly beaten
2 to 3 lb. chicken (of your choice)
2 cup of flour
1 teaspoon salt
1/4 teaspoon pepper
1/4 cup butter, melted

In a bowl, combine dressing and egg; set aside. Rinse chicken with water and drain well. Dredge chicken pieces in flour mix with salt and pepper; dip into dressing egg mixture, roll in flour again. Arrange chicken pieces in a broiler pan lined with foil. Drizzle with butter. Bake 350 degrees for 50 minutes to 1 hour or until fork tender.

Classic Cheese Burgers

This recipe can be done on both the grill or stove top for people like me who aren't grill masters

Serves 5

2 lbs. ground beef
2 tablespoons of Worcestershire sauce
1 tablespoon of canola oil
1 1/2 tablespoon Montreal steak seasoning
1/2 cup oatmeal oats
5 slices of a cheese of your choice (I like American)
5 toasted hamburger buns

In a medium sized bowl mix the ground beef, Worcestershire sauce, Montreal steak seasoning, and oatmeal together until smooth. Divide the beef into 5 equal portions, forming each portion into an inch thick patty.

For stove top

Heat oil in the pan over high heat until oil shimmers. Cook burgers until brown, about 4-5 minutes on each side. Add cheese, if using to the top of the burger, sandwich the burger between the toasted buns and serve.

For the grill

Heat a gas grill to high or heat coals in a charcoal grill until they glow bright orange and ash over. Brush the burgers with the oil. Grill the burgers until golden brown and slightly charred on the first side, about 5 minutes. Flip over the burgers. Cook beef burgers until golden brown and slightly charred on the second side, 4 minutes for medium rare or until cooked to desired degree of doneness. Add cheese, if using to the top of the burger, sandwich the burger between the toasted buns and serve.

Fried Chicken and Gravy

Now I wouldn't be very southern if I couldn't fry chicken. Nothing makes me think of the Deep South more than taking a bite of some crunchy, juicy, tender fried chicken.

1/2 cup milk
1 egg, beaten
1 cup all-purpose flour
2 teaspoons garlic salt
1 teaspoon paprika
1 teaspoon ground black pepper
1/4 teaspoon poultry seasoning
1 pound boneless skinless chicken breast,
3 cups vegetable oil
1 cup chicken broth
1 cup milk

In a medium bowl, beat together 1/2 cup milk and egg. In a resalable plastic bag, mix together the flour, garlic salt, paprika, pepper and poultry seasoning. Place chicken in bag, seal, and shake to coat. Dip chicken in milk and egg mixture, then once more in flour mixture. Reserve any remaining flour mixture.

In a large skillet, heat oil to 365 degrees F (185 degrees C). Place coated chicken in the hot oil, and brown on all sides. Reduce heat to medium-low, and continue cooking chicken until tender, about 30 minutes. Remove chicken from skillet, and drain on paper towels.

Discard all but 2 tablespoons of the frying oil. Over low heat, stir in 2 tablespoons of the reserved flour mixture. Stirring constantly, cook about 2 minutes. Whisk in chicken stock, scraping browned bits off bottom of skillet. Stir in 1 cup milk, and bring all to a boil over high heat, stirring constantly. Reduce heat to low, and simmer for about 5 minutes. Serve immediately with the chicken.

Oven Roasted Chicken Quarters

Quarters are a lot easier than a whole chicken.

Serves 2
2 chicken quarters
2 tablespoons unsalted butter melted
1 tablespoon of basil
1 tablespoon rosemary
1 tablespoon parsley
A dash of bay leaves
Salt and pepper to taste

Preheat the oven to 375 degrees. In a 13 x 9 casserole dish (I like to line my pans with foil to make less of a mess) place the chicken quarters. Pour the melted butter, rosemary, Basil, parsley, and bay leaves over top of the chicken. Cover with foil and bake for 30 minutes to an hour, half way through take the foil off and allow the chicken to finish cooking until brown and skin is crisp.

Beef Tips over Butter Noodles

3-4 lbs. stew beef
½ cup of flour
1 cup of milk
1 beef bouillon cube
Salt and pepper
1 package of egg noodles
2 sticks butter or margarine
A dash dried parsley

Brown beef and drain. Place beef a pot cover with water, bring to boil until tender. At least 2 hours. Remove beef and place in a large baking dish. In a sauce pot melt one stick of butter; add flour, milk, and beef bouillon cube. Stir until thick and creamy, pour gravy over beef salt and pepper to taste. Put in oven at 350 degrees for ½ hour to an hour, until gravy thickens

Prepare noodle according to package, drain well. Melt stick of butter and fold into the noodles. Sprinkle with parsley and ladle beef over noodles and serve.

Cheesy Potato Chili

1 Tablespoon Olive/ vegetable oil
1 lb. ground beef
Salt
Pepper
1 teaspoon dried oregano
3/4 teaspoon ground cumin
1/2 teaspoon chili powder
3/4 teaspoon cumin
1/4 paprika
3 cloves of garlic chopped
1 tablespoon tomato paste
1 extra-large potato peeled and chopped
1 diced tomato
1 cup beef or chicken stock
1 tablespoon dried cilantro
1 cup shredded cheese

Place a large non- stick heavy bottom pan over medium heat, drizzle in 1 tablespoon of oil: once hot crumble ground beef, breaking up slightly with a spoon, and brown it for 2-3 minutes. Add salt and pepper to taste, then the oregano, ground cumin, chili powder, and paprika, stir to combine. Next add garlic and tomato paste, stir and cook the mixture for a minute or two. Add the chopped potatoes and diced tomatoes, plus the chicken stock, and stir to combine; fold in the dried cilantro and about half of the shredded cheese. Serve in bowls topped with the remaining cheese.

Sides

No Bake Macaroni and Cheese

2 cups elbow macaroni
2 1/2Tbsp Butter, divide
1 ½Tbsp all-purpose flour
1 ½ cups of milk
¼ tsp salt and pepper
1 ½ cups shredded cheddar cheese
¼ cup dried bread crumbs

Cook macaroni according to package directions; drain; set aside. Melt 1 Tbsp. butter in a small skillet; add bread crumbs; cook and stir until toasted- about 3 min; set aside. In medium saucepan melt remaining butter; add flour; cook over low heat, stirring occasionally, until thickened; stir in salt and pepper. Remove pan from heat; add cheese; stir cheese until melted.

Stir macaroni into cheese sauce; spoon onto individual serving plates; sprinkle with toasted bread crumbs and serve.

Jalapeno Cornbread

Add a little heat to your everyday cornbread.

1 cup yellow cornmeal
2 teaspoons baking powder
2 large eggs
3 tablespoons sour cream
1 (8oz.) can creamed corn
5 tablespoons jalapenos, chopped into tiny bits
Olive oil cooking spray

Preheat oven to 375 degrees F. Put the cornmeal and baking powder into a large mixing bowl; make a dent in the middle that is called a well. The other ingredients go into the well. Put the eggs, sour cream and creamed corn into the well. Stir this mixture by starting with the ingredients in the. Break up the eggs, mixing the sour cream and creamed corn as you go. Then just start to fold in the dry ingredients from along the side. Add your jalapeno bits and mix once more. Grease a 9x9- inch pan with the cooking spray. Pour your corn bread mixture into the pan. Bake for 15-20 minutes. You can tell when it's when the corn bread firms up along the sides and starts to pull away. It will be a light golden color. Serve with warm butter.

Mashed Potatoes

Let's see, what would go well with both our chicken fried steak and fried chicken, and gravy? I got it mashed potatoes. Mmm! Warm creamy, buttery mashed potatoes with warm gravy drizzled over top.

Serves 2
1 pound of potatoes peeled
1/2 cup of sour cream
1-2 tablespoons of butter
Salt and pepper to taste

Place potatoes into a pot of salted water, bring to a boil and cook until tender, about 15-20 minutes, drain and place into a bowl. Using a potato masher, mash potatoes until there aren't any big chunks then using a spoon or spatula stir in milk, butter, and salt and pepper until creamy.

Drop Biscuits

A tasty and easy dinner biscuit

2 cups All-purpose flour
1/4 teaspoon salt
1 tablespoon baking powder
1/2 cup melted butter
2 teaspoons white sugar
1 cup of milk
1/2 teaspoon cream of tartar
Preheat oven to 450 degrees

In a large bowl, combine flour, baking powder, sugar, cream tartar, and salt. Stir in butter and milk just until moistened. Drop batter on a lightly greased cookie sheet by tablespoon.

Bake in preheated oven until golden on the edges. About 8-12 minutes.

Sweet Potato Casserole

3 cups sweet potatoes mashed
1/3 cup of milk
2 eggs slightly beaten
¾ cup sugar
1 teaspoon vanilla extract
½ cup butter
Topping
¾ cup brown sugar
4 tablespoon soften butter
1/3 cup flour
1 cup chopped pecans

In a large bowl blend the sweet potatoes, milk, eggs, sugar, vanilla, and butter together well. Pour into a 2qrt casserole dish and bake for 20 minutes at350 degrees

In a medium bowl mix the brown sugar, butter, flour, and pecans together until crumbly, then sprinkle onto the and bake for another 15 minutes. Allow to cool some before serving.

Green Bean Casserole

1 can (10 ¾ oz.) cream of mushroom soup
½ cup of milk
1 teaspoon soy sauce
Dash of black pepper
4 cups frozen cut green beans
1 1/3 cup French fried onion

Stir soup, milk, soy sauce, black pepper, and 2/3 cups onions in 1 ½ quart casserole dish.

Bake at 350 F for 25 minutes or until hot, stir. Top with remaining onions. Bake for 5 minutes more.

Kidney Bean Salad

2 pieces celery
2 hard-boiled eggs, chopped
2 dill pickles, diced
Mayonnaise or Italian dressing
¼ teaspoon salt
1/8 teaspoon pepper
¼ teaspoon onion powder or ¼ cup
chopped onions

Drain beans; then rinse and drain again. Combine beans with celery, egg, pickle, and all seasonings. Add mayonnaise or dressing to taste.

Sausage Cheese Balls

2 packages of uncooked ground breakfast
sausage
4 cups of shredded cheese
½ cup finely chopped onion
1 ½ cup of all-purpose flour
½ teaspoon garlic powder
½ cup finely chopped celery

Preheat oven to 375 degrees F. In a large
bowl mix sausage, cheese, onion, flour,
garlic powder, and celery, then form into
1 inch balls and place on an ungreased
baking sheet. Bake for 15 minutes or until
golden brown, makes 6 dozen.

Apple Dumplings

The best way to describe an apple dumpling is that it's a mix between an apple pie and a cobbler. It has a warm buttery, flakiness from the crescents and just the right amount of tartness from the luscious Granny Smith apple.

1 can of crescent rolls
5 Tablespoons from a stick of Margarine
1 large Granny smith apple
¾ Cup sugar
½ can sprite

Separate rolls, peel and core apple, cut into pieces. Put apple in roll, fold over. Make sure the ends are close together. Put in the microwave until rolls puff up. Don't overcook. Take out.

Melt your sugar and margarine together. This can also be done in the microwave. Pour margarine and sugar over all of the crescent rolls, and then pour ½ can of sprite over rolls. Put into oven and finish cooking until brown.

Sugar Cookies/ Homemade Icing

I enjoy sitting down with a cup of coffee and biting into a warm sugar cookie.

Cookie
3/4 cup unsalted butter or shortening
1/4 cup of water
1 3/4 cup of sugar
2 eggs
1 Teaspoon baking powder
2 eggs
4 cups of flour
1/4 teaspoon salt
2 teaspoons vanilla

Icing
1 cup powdered sugar
1 1/2 tablespoons of milk
1 teaspoon of vanilla

Preheat oven to 400 degrees F. In a separate bowl mix flour, baking powder, salt: set aside. Using an electric mixer (or spatula) cream butter and water. Add all sugar slowly and beat until smooth and creamy. Mix in vanilla. Add eggs and blend well. Add flour mixture one cup at a time. Should appear crumbly but soft to the touch. Add a touch of water if dry. Dough will not be smooth but will mash in your hand together adequately. Roll out into a thin sheet (On a slightly floured surface too much will toughen the dough) a portion at a time. Cut out as desired. Place on a pan sprayed with cooking spray. With new rolling add fresh flour to also prevent the dough from becoming tough. Bake for about 6 1/2 to 8 minutes

Depending on the oven. Before edges over brown and cookies are firm yet slightly soft. Let cool completely before removing from pan. Makes 2 dozen 5" to 6" cookies

Icing

Combine all ingredients and stir until smooth. Take a spoon or butter-knife and apply icing to cooled cookie.

York Sensational Brownies

A new way to spice up your brownie recipe

1 1/2 cups (3 sticks) butter or margarine, melted
3 cups of sugar
1 tablespoon vanilla extract
2 cups all-purpose flour
1 cup Hershey's cocoa
5 eggs
1 teaspoon baking powder
1 teaspoon salt
24 small (1 1/2 inch) York Peppermint Patties, unwrapped

Preheat oven 350 degrees (If using a glass pan, 325 degrees). Grease a 13x9x2-inch baking pan. In a large bowl with spoon, or wire whisk. Stir together butter, sugar, and vanilla. Add eggs; stir until well blended. Stir in, flour, cocoa, baking powder, and salt; blend well. Reserve 2 cups of batter; set aside. Spread remaining batter in prepared pan. Arrange peppermint patties in a single layer over the batter, about a 1/2-inch apart. Spread reserved 2 cups of batter over the patties. Bake 50 to 55 minutes or until brownies pull away from the sides of the pan. Cool completely in pan or wire rack; cut into squares.

Apple Crisp

¼ cup of sugar
1 teaspoon cinnamon
1 tablespoon of cornstarch
Pinch of salt
8 cups granny smith apples (peeled, cored, and sliced)
2/3 cups regular oats
½ cup brown sugar
1 tablespoon of flour
¼ cup butter, melted

Combine sugar, cinnamon, cornstarch, and salt in a large bowl, mix well. Place the apples in an 8x8 baking dish. Sprinkle with the sugar mixture. Combine oats, brown sugar, and flour and sprinkle over apples. Drizzle butter over apple mixture and bake for 30 minutes 400 degrees.

Chocolate Chip Cookies

Nothing warms my heart or stomach more than a warm, chewy, melt in your mouth chocolate chip cookie.

2 ½ cup all-purpose flour
1 teaspoon baking soda
1 ½ cups brown sugar
1 egg
¾ cups margarine melted and cooled
2 teaspoon vanilla extract
1 cup semi-sweet chocolate chips

Preheat the oven to 350. Combine flour and baking soda. Set aside. In a large bowl, combine melted margarine stick and brown sugar. Mix well. Stir in egg and vanilla extract until well blended. Add flour mixture and stir until just combined. Stir in chocolate chips. For each drop a heaping tablespoon of dough onto a cookie sheet, leaving about 2 ½ inches between each bake at 350 for 9 to 11 minutes.

No Egg Key Lime Pie

For all of you wonderful people who can't have eggs I have a tasty treat for you.

1 can condensed milk
1/2 cup key lime juice (approx.)
8 oz. cream cheese
12 oz. Cool whip whipped cream
2 prepared pie shells (pre-baked or graham cracker)

Blend milk and cream cheese until smooth. Add lime juice and mix thoroughly. Add thawed cool whip. Pour into the pie shells. Garnish with lime rind (optional) and refrigerate for 6 hours.

Pistachio Salad

1 package of Pistachio instant pudding
1 can crushed pineapple
8 oz. of cool whip
1 cup mini marshmallow
1 cup crushed pecans

In a bowl mix pudding mixes with crushed pineapples. Fold in container of cool whip; add marshmallows, and pecans. Mix well and refrigerate until ready to serve.

Zucchini Banana Nut Bread

1 1/4 cups all-purpose flour
1 teaspoon baking soda
1/2 teaspoon salt
2 large eggs
1 teaspoon vanilla extract
1 stick of butter
3 very ripe Bananas
1/2 cup chopped pecan
1/2 cup shredded or chopped zucchini

Sift flour, baking soda, and salt into a medium bowl and set aside. Whisk eggs and vanilla together in a liquid measuring cup with a spout and set aside. Lightly spray a 9x5x3 inch bread pan with non-stick spray. Preheat oven to 350°F. In cream butter and sugar until light and fluffy. Gradually add the egg mixture, and then add the bananas and zucchini. Add the flour mixture until just incorporated. Then fold in pecans and transfer to bread pan. Bake for 55 to 60 minutes

About the Author

Emily Roberts was born in the small town of Monroe, Louisiana born on September 28, 1992.

Emily and her husband recently moved to the beautiful hill country of Missouri; and recently gave birth to their first child. Emily loves cooking and baking from scratch. Emily also enjoys inventing as well as reinventing recipes passed down from generation to generation.